What's your dream job

A Complete Guide to Landing Your Dream Job, Building a World-Class Personal Brand, and Achieving Success in Business and Life

North DEAN

The information herein is offered for informational purposes solely and is universal as so. The presentation of the information is without a contract or any type of guarantee assurance.

The trademarks that are used are without any consent, and the publication of the trademark is without permission or backing by the trademark owner. All trademarks and brands within this book are for clarifying purposes only and are the owned by the owners themselves, not affiliated with this document.

Table of Content

Introduction

Chapter 1: Why Isn't It Working For You?

Chapter 2: Know Yourself

Chapter 3: Know Your Skills

Chapter 4: Build Your Project

Chapter 5: Build Your Brand

Chapter 6: Break Free

Chapter 7: Enjoy Your Success (Conclusion)

Introduction

- *Are you a job seeker searching for the job of your dreams?*
- *Do you have a job, but you deeply want that promotion you know you deserve?*
- *Do you want to advance your career and do work that makes you feel passionate and purposeful?*

Then look no further: In this book, I'll give you a step-by-step guide to help you live a lifetime of meaningful work.

This book will first help you work on yourself and give you advice on self-assessment and self-awareness. From there, it will walk you through practical tools and strategies you can use to achieve career success.

To be a bit more specific, this book will cover and teach you the following:

- *The ins and outs of self-assessment to help you design your career—and your life—around your passions, transferable skills, traits, and more,*

- *Powerful job-hunting strategies that work,*

- *How to build an effective online resume,*

- *How to leverage social media for success,*

- *How to build your brand and network effectively to achieve the success you desire,*

- *And so much, much more.*

Essentially, this guide aims to provide you, whether you're a new graduate, job-hunter, and career changer, with tools you can use to discover—and land—your dream job.

Before we dive deep into it, you might be wondering who I am and what experience I have to teach you any of these things. Well:

A little bit about me

I started my work career as a first-level techy. From hard work, I then moved on to a C-Level Position in various multinational companies, became a sought-after consultant, and then a top-tier executive.

My hands-on experience means I know a thing or two about career development and fulfillment. Along the way, I've also become a personal branding and digital strategy expert.

Like most people:

I've been through my fair share of deception and limitations in terms of my career. After 11 years of loyal service to my employers, I never got the promotion I believe I deserved.

However, instead of letting down and giving in, I

invested thousands of dollars into personal development training, coaching programs, and career development.

This book shares what I've learned from these investments: *potent career success secrets you can implement right now to get yourself on the path to living a meaningful life and building your dream career.*

Another question you may have is, *"Why have you chosen now to share this information?"*

Well:

As I write this, the economy is shifting, and more and more people are getting laid off; you might be a victim yourself, and I'm so sorry you had to go through that if you are.

As you might know, Digital Transformation is rendering most jobs obsolete, causing many people to get laid off.

Besides this, most people want jobs that, in addition to paying well, have missions that inspire, motivate them, and give them a sense of purpose and usefulness to society.

Whatever reasons you may have for seeking career growth, this book has practical advice that will help you start living the career life you desire.

To get the most out of this book, I strongly recommend putting into practice the various exercises we shall discuss in various parts of this book because **growth takes action.**

With that stated, let's dive in:

CHAPTER 1

WHY ISN'T IT WORKING FOR YOU?

Having the life you desire and a career to boot is not only for the chosen few. The truth is that, although there are some limitations, anyone can build their dream career and life. The key is to identify precisely why things don't seem to be working for you and then determine how to go about making them work for you.

*The Dream Position
You Didn't Get*

Let's assume that there's an opening for the head of sales and you've always wanted this position. You know you want it, badly at that, but instead of putting your hat into the ring or asking for the job, you cross your fingers and hope you get the position.

Unfortunately, the job goes to Jeff, who seemed to have scheduled a meeting with the boss two days before the boss pronounced him as the new head of sales. In the end, the question that plagues your mind is, *"Why couldn't I have done that?"*

Well:

Voice-Up

If you want something, you have to ask for it: there is no other way around it if you want to advance your career. Your boss wants to see that you have the drive and confidence to go after what you want.

Speaking up goes beyond asking for the promotion of your dreams; you also need to speak up at meetings so that your boss knows you have good ideas. Remember: your boss can't read your mind.

If you are not used to speaking up about what you want, this might sound easier said than done, but it's something you have to do if you want career growth.

Here're some simple, practical tips you can work on to overcome voice-up issues:

How to get your voice heard: Simple, practical tips

Before pumping yourself up to speak, there is one key factor you need to consider before speaking up at work regardless of the situation: *do your homework!*

Preparation gives you confidence; it helps you know what to say and how to say it.

If you want to speak up about that dream position, you need to prepare adequately before scheduling that meeting with your boss. At the most basic level, you will need to research the following:

- **The job description:** What does the role entails, and which responsibilities come with it?

- **Your strengths, skills, and qualifications:** What makes you the best person for the job?

- **Reasons for promotion:** Why do you deserve that promotion? Ensure you play with facts, not just words. If you are in sales, you could say something like, "Last year, I progressively increased my sales by a minimum of 10% each month."

- Lastly, don't be afraid to tell your boss that

> you genuinely and deeply want that promotion; a little honesty and passion go a long way.

Have you ever had that creeping feeling that you don't deserve your job despite your accomplishments? Have you ever felt like you aren't good enough to succeed?

If yes, you might have a case of *imposter syndrome*, something you need to overcome:

You Are Not an Imposter

Imposter syndrome is a psychological phenomenon experienced by people at any level or industry. It is a feeling of inadequacy that makes you feel that you won't experience success—or are undeserving of it —and quite frankly, it can get you stuck. According to research conducted by the International Journal of Behavioral Science,[1] 70% of people experience this syndrome at some point in their lives.

If you've fallen into this trap, don't beat yourself up; the imposter syndrome forms from an accumulation of insecurities that may arise from feeling stuck in your career.

How The Imposter Syndrome Develops

The imposter syndrome is triggered by a stressor, which is usually a new opportunity or success. It could be a new job, obtaining a degree, or any other significant milestones in your career.

When you achieve this significant success, you start having negative thoughts that make you feel that you didn't earn the success you achieved. We call such thoughts' *cognitive distortions,'* thoughts based on anxiety and fear, not facts.

For instance:

When you're applying for a new job, you might start

telling yourself that the achievements on your resume are flukes or how unqualified you are. These thoughts may leave you feeling worried that the interviewing panel will call you out for "being an imposter."

The imposter syndrome is nothing but a collection of beliefs formed from repetition. The good news is that you can overcome the imposter syndrome and get back your confidence and drive.

How To Overcome The Imposter Syndrome

To beat this syndrome:

#: Do a reality check

We put ourselves down many times, especially when faced with a setback. When you experience such moments, it's always a good idea to stop and remember just who we are, what you have accomplished, what you're capable of achieving.

Think about all your significant accomplishments and consider how you felt at that particular time. Whenever you feel the imposter in you creeping up, remind yourself of the limitless potential within you, then focus on your most significant wins to remind yourself that you can achieve all your goals when you put in diligent, hard work.

#: Keep an eye on your negative thoughts

If you think your coworkers didn't invite you to lunch because they think you are clueless, then this is a negative thought, and you have to realize that it's just that, a thought.

When such a thought comes to mind, acknowledge it and look for reasons why it might be popping up. You could say something like, *"I'm having this thought because I'm not feeling so confident, but the truth is, I'm well educated, and I have sufficient experience. I work hard, and I'm good at what I do."*

#: List your accomplishments

In addition to reminding yourself of your accomplishments, create a list of your accomplishments, strengths, and skills that qualify you for the job you want. Have this list at the ready for moments when you are having a bad day.

If you have a vision board with your goals, make sure your board has a list of what makes you different and unique from other people. You can also write down any positive feedback you've gotten from the people around you. That can give you a clear picture of where you are succeeding and where you need to put in extra effort to develop.

#: Create a support network at work

You can never underestimate the power of social connections. Those feeling like imposters usually isolate themselves, which is the worst thing they can do.

Self-isolation usually happens because the imposter syndrome causes you to assume the worst, which keeps you from seeking validation and accurate feedback from other people.

The upside to social interactions is that people can normalize your experiences and ascertain that your thoughts about yourself aren't accurate. You will not only need to nurture your relationships with coworkers but also with your boss.

You don't have to wait for the annual performance review to interact with them. It can be as simple as asking for feedback on what you are doing well and what you need to improve. Your boss will appreciate that you are inquisitive and invested enough to know how you can do better.

Once you have a trusted network, you won't be afraid to ask for guidance from your coworkers when you feel stuck. Don't hesitate to go for those lunches and catch a beer after work with the team.

#: Work on your knowledge reserve

It's simple here:

The more you learn about your job and industry at large, the more you feel confident about what you are doing and the more power you have—knowledge is power, literally.

One great place you can get such comprehensive information is Monster for free.[2] This platform gives you access to job search tips, career advice, and workplace insights.

Although these tips seem simple, they work if you're willing to implement them diligently. As I mentioned earlier, growth and success require action.

Why Head-Hunters Ignore You

The world is full of opportunities, and in this digital era, it is considerably easy to tap into such opportunities.

Unfortunately, most people miss these opportunities because of:

Poor Or No Online Presence

Being a ghost online makes you invisible, even to employers.

According to an annual survey by CareerBuilder's[3] regarding social media recruitment, 35% of employers have a lower chance of interviewing applicants they can't find online.

Moreover, when you're a ghost online, besides the lowered possibilities of employers hiring you, you also miss chances such as job posts, career advancement programs, networking, etc.

One way to land the job of your dreams and achieve career growth and progression is to make yourself visible to the world using different online profiles, including professional platforms such as:

- LinkedIn[4]
- Xing[5]
- Bark[6]

- Opportunity Network[7]
- Jobcase[8]

Other than these, you can also use social media platforms, such as Twitter, Facebook, and Instagram, to showcase your skills.

Bad E-Reputation

Again, your online presence can also work against you. Here's how:

#: Non updated historical data

Maybe you joined LinkedIn years ago just after you graduated and have never logged in to update your experiences. Potential employers will likely pass on you, thinking you don't have the qualifications they desire, yet you might be the perfect fit.

#: Different profiles

This can be an honest mistake where you created an account, forgot you did—or forgot your logins —, and created another profile altogether. Having different profiles where you maybe have represented yourself differently can scream red flags to potential employers.

#: Careless posts

Potential employers are bound to go through your profiles; keep in mind that they have access to whatever you post online. Ideally, avoid potentially offensive posts that could come off as gender-biased, racially insensitive, politically incorrect, etc.

If this seems like a lot, don't worry. This book will guide you through a self-transformation journey that will lead you towards landing your dream job and building the career and life you aspire for and want.

CHAPTER 2

KNOW YOURSELF

"The first thing you have to know is yourself. A man who knows himself can step outside himself and watch his reactions like an observer."[9]

ADAM SMITH, THE MONEY GAME

Understanding what matters to you is critical to your career success journey. Do you know why?
Because to explore career ideas and steps to take, you must know your strengths, interests, skills, values, and, most importantly, personality. Your personality determines the actions you take and your approach.

What Makes Your Character?

Self-awareness forces you to see yourself objectively, which allows you to make adjustments that can help you move forward towards your career success and dream life.

When it comes to your career development, knowing yourself can entail examining your weaknesses, failures, strengths, and accomplishments from your past, all of which can help you move forward with fresh career objectives, re-energized goals, and better strategies.

So, where do you start? By understanding your personality better:

The Three States Of Ego Transactional Analysis

The transactional analysis is a theory established in the 1950s explaining human behavior.

This theory helps us understand that what happened in our childhood and the treatment we received from our parents, guardians, etc., still subconsciously affects how we act and think in our present. This theory states that all that notwithstanding, you are responsible for your future.

Our personalities consist of the following parts (ego

states):

1: Parent Ego State ("exteropsyche")

"Exteropsyche" revolves around the behavior, set of feelings, and way of thinking we have adapted from our significant others and parents. In essence, it encompasses your ingrained absorbed conditioning, the innate voice of authority, attitudes, and learning from when you were young.

As you grow up, you take in beliefs and behaviors from your caretakers and parents. You might notice that you are doing things or saying them just the way your mother/father/grandparents used to (even if you don't want to). We call introjecting.

What have you introjected into your personality? Indicate below:

Introjection	Personality
"My dad used to sit me down when there was an issue, and he would talk calmly about it until we figured out a resolution."	*"I dislike screaming confrontations and prefer calm talks."*

2: Child Ego State ("archaeopsyche")

These are feelings, thoughts, and sets of behaviors replayed from your childhood. Have you ever had your stomach churn after the boss called you into his office, wondering if you are in trouble? If you explored this, you might remember being called in by the principal and getting scolded.

Both the child and the parent ego get continuously updated. The child represents feelings and emotions that accompanied external events, and when despair or anger dominates reason, the child is in control.

Do you know of ways your inner child comes to play? Indicate here:

....

....

....

....

....

....

....

....

....

....

....

....

....

....

....

3: Adult Ego State ("neopsyche")

This state represents our direct responses in the present. How we deal with the things happening in our present draws heavily from our past—in a healthy manner.

In this state, we can see people for who they are instead of what we project onto them. Instead of making assumptions and staying scared, we ask for real information.

This stage is an integration of the positive aspects of our child and parent ego. If you are to change aspects of your Child and Parent, you have to do this through your Adult.

How do you showcase your adult ego? Indicate here:

....

....

....

....

....

....

....

....

....

....

....

NORTH DEAN

....

....

....

....

....

Key Principals: FIRO-B/MBTI

To understand your personality further and better, you can use the following tools:

Fundamental Interpersonal Relations Orientation (Firo-B)

FIRO-B is an assessment used to measure the extent to which people strive to satisfy the three primary social needs:

- **Inclusion:** Recognition, participation, and belonging
- **Control:** Authority, influence, and power
- **Affection:** Closeness, openness, and warmth

These three factors comprise the major areas that determine one's personality. Hence, their assessment can give you a pretty good idea of your personality, especially as it relates to your career.

The following two factors also modify each of the areas specified above:

- **Wanted behavior:** This relates to the level at which we desire others to exhibit a particular behavior towards us.
- **Expressed behavior:** In contrast, this re-

lates to how comfortable we are about expressing a specific behavior towards others.

When you apply these two factors, you end up with the six main sections of this test. These include:

1. **Expressed inclusion:** This shows the level to which you make efforts towards including others and also to get others to include you. The higher the score, the more you want to engage socially.

2. **Wanted inclusion:** This is your need to belong and your desire to have others include you without instigating it. A high score means you want others to invite you to large social groups.

3. **Expressed control:** This shows the extent of your comfort with influencing others and your efforts to control a situation. A higher score shows your comfort with taking responsibility and organizing.

4. **Wanted control:** This shows your comfort with having someone else in charge and having someone influence the direction of your actions.

5. **Expressed affection:** This shows the degree to which you try and engage others on a personal level. A high score means you are comfortable with being open and sup-

porting others.

6. **Wanted affection:** This shows you how comfortable you are with having other people take a liking to you and being warm with you in general. A high score means you are comfortable with others sharing personal things with you.

You can use the following free resources to take the FIRO-B test:

https://testets.com/pages/Career-Test-FIRO-B-BRAND.php [10]

https://careertestswork.com/mycareer/index.php?main_page=take_free [11]

DISCLAIMER: These **ARE NOT** affiliate links. I do not earn a commission from recommending these or any other resources in this book. They're just resources I think can be helpful to you; that's all!

Mbti: Myers-Briggs Type Indicator

The MBTI test is another great tool you can use to determine your personality. MBTI is a self-report inventory made to define a person's strengths, preferences, and personality type.

Here's an overview of the test:

According to this test, people can have one of 16 personality types. The test itself consists of 4 different scales:

1: Extraversion (E) – Introversion (I)

This dichotomy describes how people interact and respond to the world around them.

Extraverts, also called extroverts, are "outward-turning." They're usually action-oriented and enjoy frequent social interactions.

In contrast, introverts are "inward-turning." They're more thought-oriented and feel energized by spending time alone.

Even when we have both personalities, one is always dominant.

2: Sensing (S) – Intuition (N)

This describes how people gather information from the world around them.

For sensing, you pay great attention to reality and what you can learn from your details—from facts and details. For intuition, you rely more on impressions and patterns and enjoy thinking about possibilities.

3: Thinking (T) – Feeling (F)

This section focuses on making decisions from the information gathered. If you prefer thinking, you usually put more emphasis on objective data and facts.

If you prefer feeling, you consider people and emotions more when coming up with conclusions.

4: Judging (J) – Perceiving (P)

This is the final scale; it shows how people deal with the outside world. If you lean towards judging, you prefer firm decisions and structure. If you are more of a perceiving person, you are more adaptable, flexible, and open.

These four scales give us the following sixteen personalities:

1. ISTJ - The Inspector
2. INFJ - The Advocate
3. ISTP - The Crafter
4. ISFP - The Artist
5. INTJ - The Architect
6. INTP - The Thinker
7. INFP - The Mediator
8. ISFJ - The Protector
9. ENTJ - The Commander
10. ESTP - The Persuader
11. ESFP - The Performer
12. ESFJ - The Caregiver
13. ENFP - The Champion

14. ESTJ - The Director

15. ENFJ - The Giver

16. ENTP - The Debater

Even without taking the official questionnaire, you can already recognize some of your traits from the four different scales. You can use the following sites to conduct the Myers-Briggs self-assessment test:

https://www.16personalities.com/free-personality-test [12]

https://www.mbtionline.com/en-US/Products/For-you [13]

Understanding Your Drivers

What makes you do what you do? Do you know what gets you up every morning and keeps you going throughout the day?

Motivation, or drive, is what urges you to do what you do, making the big question, *"do you know what drives you?"*

Kahler's Five Drivers

These drivers were identified by Taibi Kahler back in 1975. The drivers are instilled in our unconsciousness and can lead to some very positive and negative behaviors. They include:

1: Be Perfect

If you feel driven by the need to be perfect, you draw energy from doing things perfectly and producing accurate work with high standards. You tend to come off as overly critical because you insist on having everything done perfectly.

The major drawback to this drive is that you are prone to missing deadlines because you'll still be checking your work.

Best suited for: Jobs where setting standards and fine detail are essential.

2: Be Strong

With this drive, you can stay calm in literally any circumstance. Your drive is the need to cope with difficult people and crises. You happily take charge of situations, and people are comfortable and feel safe to have you in charge.

Best suited for: Such a personality is excellent at putting up with things most would find unreasonable and adjusting to poor working conditions.

3: Hurry Up

With this style, you are driven by having deadlines to meet, and you always seem to be able to fit in extra work. However, when given time, you may delay working on the project until it is urgent, which can backfire because when working hastily, you're prone to making mistakes.

Best suited for: Tasks that have deadlines you need to meet, and the task's nature can change over time.

4: Please Others

If you have this drive, you are very understanding. You usually use intuition and can notice body language and other signals that other people may not see. You are often the mortar that holds together your team, but you also worry a lot about approval from other people that you are unwilling to challenge anyone's ideas, even when you know they're wrong.

Best suited for: 'Maintenance' functions such as checking and summarizing, involving people, and being empathetic and tolerant to other people's needs.

5: Try Hard

With this drive, you feel energized by having a new thing to try out. You also turn small projects into big ones since you want to chase down every responsibility. You are a natural and enthusiastic problem-solver.

Best suited for: Difficult and time-consuming situations that require persistence.

Again, you can use the following links to assess your drivers:

https://www.surveymonkey.co.uk/r/stressedatwork [14]

http://www.totem consulting.com/wp-content/uploads/2016/02/Drivers-Questionaire-1.pdf[15]

Regardless of your personality/drive, it is essential to know that there is no "one good personality" and others bad. The only value to this information is helping you get to know who you are and leverage this information to your advantage.

CHAPTER 3

KNOW YOUR SKILLS

Besides knowing your personality, knowing your skills is also essential for advancing your career and living the life you want. When you identify your skills and what you can do well, you become capable of knowing which job will suit you best and what you will enjoy doing most without it feeling strenuous.

Know-how

It's critical to be as detailed as possible about any skill you have used in your previous experiences, whatever those experiences may be.

Try to provide a skill pillar tag to each of your sets of skills. For instance, you can categories them into these categories—but don't limit yourself; this is just an example to help you out:

Skills	Operational	Technical	Functional	Personal Know-How
1.				
2.				
3.				
4.				
5.				
6.				
7.				
8.				

You can also take things a step further and indicate an example of how you've utilized that skill—to have a practical application in mind.

Attitude

You certainly have different attitudes for the different companies you've worked for and also for the different jobs and projects you've had. Mark each of the attitudes you have had corresponding to each company you've worked in throughout your career.

The different types of attitude include:

- **Character attitude:** Autonomous, Agile, open, sociable, capable of taking a step back and reflect on things.

- **Learning attitude:** Curious, taking initiatives, trying new things.

- **Behavioral attitude:** Helpful, responsible, get fully invested in a professional project.

You could have something like:

My attitude in company A

....
....
....
....
....
....

My attitude in company B:

....
....
....
....
....
....
....
....

My Attitude Towards Project A

....
....
....
....
....
....

My Attitude Towards Project B:

....
....
....
....
....
....

Space for indicating your attitude:

Attitude/skills	Enjoyed	Didn't enjoy	Desire to use	Don't desire to use	Encountered and want to improve further
1.					
2.					
3.					

Management

You can also use the same process you used to identify your skills to identify your management skills.

- *What's your core leadership style?*

- *How well do you relate with your team?*

- *What does your team say about you and your leadership?*

Answers to these questions can give you a good idea of your management skills.

It doesn't matter if you don't have any management experience. If you aspire to be in a managerial role at some point in your career, be honest with yourself and state what would describe you most as a manager.

You can indicate your management skills below:

....

....

....

....

....

....

....

Your Knowledge Pyramid

Now get back to your Know-how list that you have already prepared and count the skills according to each pillar tag you have determined. The most prevailing one will be on top of the pyramid (that is your strongest skillset), the second most important on the right, and the last on the left of the pyramid's baseline.

Create a pyramid such as the one below:

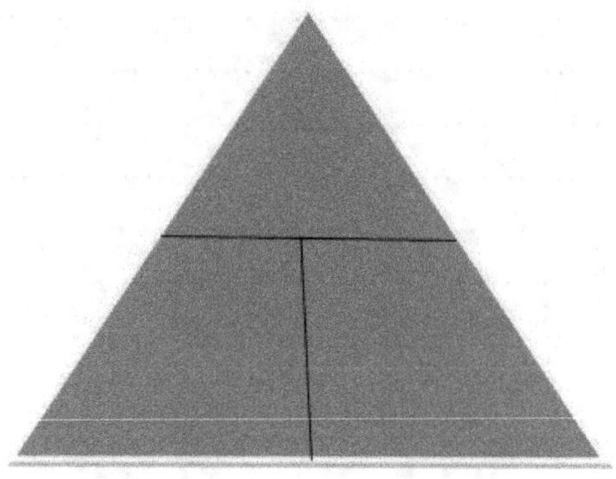

Indicate your skills in each section as explained above.

Congratulations! You now have a visual aspect of your skillset, know-how, and competencies that will help you build your future career and life success project:

CHAPTER 4

BUILD YOUR PROJECT

After understanding yourself and your capabilities better, the next step is to build your project, which, in this case, is your dream career and life.

Before we discuss how to do this in practice, you have to prepare your mindset also. How you think reflects your actions; therefore, working on your mindset is essential to any successful project:

Get the Right Mindset

Have you ever asked yourself what sets apart those who achieve great things from those who don't realize their ambitions? If you think it's intelligence, creativity, or a risk appetite, you are wrong—although these are sensible suggestions.

According to Stanford psychologist Carol Dweck and other researchers, your mindset[16] is the major predictor of success in life.

Mindset refers to your collection of beliefs and thoughts that shape your thought process. Therefore, having the right mindset means shaping a healthy way of thinking.

Cultivating the right mindset involves:

Having An Abundance Mindset

You might see the term abundance and think "excess," but an abundance mindset isn't about excess stuff. It is about having a deep feeling of satisfaction in your mind and soul.

Such a mindset can keep you going even if things aren't going so well for you. You will need this as you work hard to achieve career growth and success since, as you do, you are bound to encounter challenges at one point or another.

From another perspective, abundance in your career development means being capable of seeing opportunities everywhere. There is no such thing as a saturated job market. There are plenty of opportunities and dream positions out there; we just need to prepare ourselves to meet them.

Some of the ways to cultivate this mindset include:

#: Practice Gratitude

There's no better way to cultivate an abundance mindset than being grateful for what you already have.

Take some time every day to come up with at least five things you are grateful for, especially related to your job and career in general. Don't worry if you can't come up with career-related things you are grateful for; you can also write down what you are grateful for generally.

Read aloud what you've written and take time to feel genuine gratitude. If you don't get an instant feeling of contentment, you can hit me up and tell me that it didn't work—seriously,(I will provide my contact information at the end of the book).

PS: Save these lists so you can go through them when you are not feeling so motivated.

#: Practicing positivity

It is hard to stay positive all the time, especially when facing hardships and challenges. However, it can be such a great stress reliever.

Whenever a thought or something negative comes to mind, counter it with something positive. If you get hurt and are on your way to the ER, think about how fortunate you are to live in a country with quick emergency services. If you don't get that promotion, think about the extra time you now have to perfect your skill and be more efficient once you get the position.

In other words, every situation, yes, even the worst-seeming, has a related positive aspect; you only have to be willing to look for it as diligently as you can.

#: A giving heart

Giving doesn't necessarily have to mean tangible, luxurious gifts or money. You can offer people your time, energy, positivity, kindness, and even home-made gifts, something meaningful to the other person.

If you can give out a $10,000 check to charity, then well and good. However, if you can't, you can always volunteer, buy a meal for someone in need, offer a listening ear, get someone flowers to brighten up their day, etc.

Success Mindset

A success mindset is a winning mindset that keeps you going when you feel like defeat is inevitable. If you have such a mindset, you have a clear picture of the steps you'll take to achieve your goals, and you aren't afraid to fail. As long as you know you are doing things the right way, you will keep going.

To cultivate a success-oriented mindset, you need to:

#: Understand that you need to put in the work

To be successful, you have to put in the effort whether you like it or not- and this is what a success mindset calls for, *effort*!

That promotion won't just come to you; you will have to work for it. The excellent relationship you want with your boss won't happen magically; you will have to work to make it happen. Whatever you want to achieve can only come to you through action. There is no other way!

Whatever your goals are, start taking action now. It doesn't matter how small the action is; the important thing is to do something that moves you forward!

#: Don't go all in

Small incremental steps are the way to go. Diving all in might seem like a good idea because it's quick and might realize results faster, but it is seldom the right thing to do. Besides, focusing on doing that big thing all at once might delay your progress, and you might never begin.

For instance:

If you want to invest in real estate, you might want to start with small listings and work your way up to the big fish. If you focus on the big fish from the word go, you might never make your investments.

#: Always consider yourself as WIP (Work in Progress)

You can never stop making yourself better; no matter how much you've grown, developed, and succeeded, there's always room for improvement. Businesses are all about solving real-world problems for their consumers; you need to ensure your skills are always up to date.

Sign up for anything and everything whenever you have the time; you never know when it will come in handy.

#: Revamp and readjust your goals

Nothing is ever certain in this ever-changing world we live in, and so, your goals shouldn't be static either. If you feel you need to readjust your goals to suit your plans and efforts, don't hesitate or be afraid to do so. Change is the only constant thing in life. Remember, as long as you know what you are doing, trust your methods.

Navigating Change Skillfully

For this section, we will be using the lifeLine technique, a simple system that can empower you and help you become more conscious and aware of the resources that can motivate and keep you progressing.

At the most basic level, a LifeLine is a simple chart representing key events and ups and downs that have significantly influenced your career and life. This chart can help you gain insight into future career choices and help you begin thinking about what you might want to change or develop and do next.

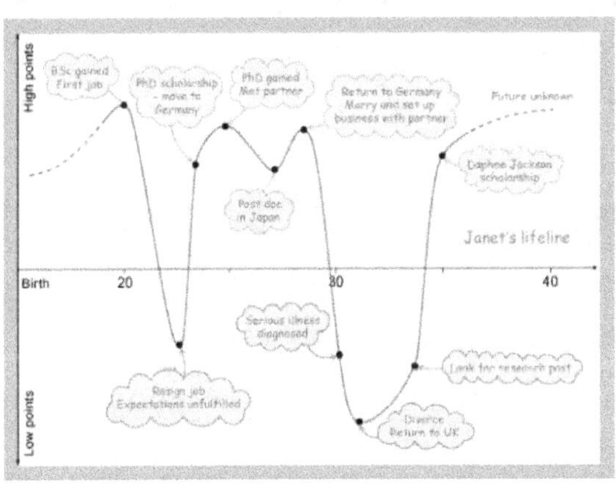

FIG 1: SAMPLE LIFELINE CHART FROM OPENLEARN[17]

Exercise 1

Create a similar LifeLine chart.

All you need to do is draw a line and start with your birth date on one end and today's date on the other end. On your LifeLine, be sure to highlight all the important life events as well as transitions, your personal high points, and times when you struggled. Place them as shown in the sample, with the best highlights having the highest points.

Give examples of resources you called upon and used during those life challenges—they can also be personal values. Make sure to keep the ones that have been the most useful to you. Be sure to focus on the emotions you felt and the ones you feel now as you recall these events.

Resource Analysis

Most of the time, we find out that we have achieved more than what we think we have; we just haven't reflected enough on it (let's be proud of it!).

The LifeLine technique calls on you to choose an event and place a number in front of each resource —or multiple resources—you have called upon to achieve something or overcome a difficulty. The highest numbers will represent your strongest inner resource that you need to be aware of and tap into to achieve greater life and career success. Assess this below:

Determine Your Dream Job

First, congratulations, you have made it to this part of the book. That shows how serious you are about your career and life success/project. Before we determine your dream job, let's talk about goals for a bit.

Your Goals And Objectives

Do you set goals on New Year, but by the end of January, you can't even recall where you wrote them down? I hope not!

Goals and objectives are vital to success, and without them, it is easy to lose direction. Here is a very, very small sampling of reasons why goals are so integral to success:

- **Goals keep you focused:** Goals help you zero in on what you need to do each day to achieve what you want to do in a month. They keep you focused on the milestones you need to achieve daily to fulfill your weekly and monthly goals.

- **They can help you assess your progress and stay motivated:** There's nothing as satisfying as ticking things off your goal lists. It is easy to feel discouraged, especially when working towards something big, but

> you feel motivated to keep going when you see your progress through goals achieved and items ticked off your list.
>
> - **Goals give you a taste of victory:** You can't taste victory once and not want to taste it again. Goals make you want to achieve more and more, which can push you to levels you never thought you'd reach.

Given all this, if you haven't set goals yet, it's about time you did. You can categorize your goals into these categories—again, don't limit yourself:

- Short-term goals
- Long-term goals
- Lifetime goals

Now that you have an idea about your goals and a holistic view of your personality traits, drivers/motivators, skills, and resourcefulness, let's align all these to define your dream job.

Exercise 2

Come up with a list of 5 dream jobs/positions you are aspiring for and follow the Sample template below to guide you in your decision (assign the values to the personalities and drivers based on the job description requirements and assess your suitability).

Dream job	Personality	Driver\motivator	Compatibility %
Sales Executive	ISTP	Hurry up	80%
	ISFJ	Be perfect	60%
Executive Assistant	ESFJ	Try hard	90%
	ENTP	Please others	70%
Manager	ENTJ	Be strong	90%
	ENFJ	Please others	50%
CFO (Chief Financial Office)	INTP	Be perfect	80%
	ESFJ	Try hard	80%
CMO (Chief Marketing Office)	ENFP	Be perfect	90%
	ESTJ	Hurry up	70%

Fill your personalized assessment below. You can also add the following fields to make your assessment as accurate as possible, but don't limit yourself to these categories; you can add anything else you deem fit:

Dream Job	Preferred salary	Location of the job	Its mission	Industry	Size of the company

Take your time on doing this exercise and explore different possibilities; By the end of the exercise, you should come up with a list of the top three jobs with the highest scores; the one with the highest score will be your primary go-to target job.

Sometimes reaching your dream job requires an intermediary transition; remember, be realistic about your goals and capabilities. If this is the case, try to go to the next job on your top three jobs list and start working for it while giving yourself the time and the means to reach your final goal. From my personal experience: Before I get named as a Chief information officer, I had to accept a transitory role as head of operations and be named deputy of the actual CIO. It took one year, but I ended up in the position, and guess what? Having spent that year as a deputy allowed me to understand better the job challenges, the company culture, and how to be very successful in my target role.

CHAPTER 5

BUILD YOUR BRAND

Now that you have found your path, I will show you how to make the world know about it and become an authority in your field.

In this digitalized world of ours, it makes sense to build your brand online; everyone and every organization operate this way, and this is the only way to make yourself visible in the business world.

The fact that we've determined your resources is excellent, but now you need to reach the right audience, make people know about you, and build market trust, which is essential to building a successful brand.

Why You Should Build Your Brand Online (A Vibrant Online Presence)

Your personal brand and how you define and control it is essential to career success. Regardless of whether you are searching for an employer or clients for your business, you need to present yourself out there so that people can see and find you; your potential clients and employers are all online waiting for you.

In this digital era, companies want the best in terms of skills and image. Knowing how to communicate your expertise will help companies understand what you do and what you are all about, setting you as the hidden gem businesses are looking to hire as fast as possible.

If you are a freelancer or work in a home office, building your brand sets you as an authority in your field.

The online world is nothing more than an extension of who we are; your social media amplifies you. People judge you by the content you post online, and if you are a ghost online, they judge that too. Thus, having an online presence that works for you is your best bet.

Remember that the online world isn't going anywhere; actually, it will only get more versatile. Thus, getting on board and being an expert sailor should be your goal.

Navigating Social Media

No matter which social media platform you want to use or are using, you need to know how to navigate it to build your brand. Ideally, you will need to:

#: Know your audience

Are you targeting clients, employers, or employees? What's your target's group age range, preferences, choice of platform, etc. The more targeted your social media efforts are, the more effective they will be.

#: Consistency

The thing about social media is that people move on fast. Have you ever seen something trend like a day but become wholly forgotten the next day?

To avoid falling into that trap, you need to feed your audience with constant content so that you don't become obsolete. Keep your profile updated with your latest work and information.

#: Do your research

Never post about something that you don't have complete facts on; doing so could utterly backfire on you, even when you thought you were on the right side.

Always fact-check anything you want to post, ALWAYS. Doing this is especially important if whatever you are posting will call for the opinions of other people. Again when it comes to research, it always helps to research the best strategies to implement to make sure your efforts bear fruit.

E-Reputation

E-reputation, or online reputation, is your digital identity that is on the internet and digital platforms.

As we have established, your online presence is essential to your personal growth and career growth. Hence, having a positive online reputation should be one of your goal list.

Impact Of A Bad E-Reputation

Going by the CareerBuilder study[18] of 2017, 70% of employers go through their candidate's social media profiles, and 69% Google their candidates as part of the applicant screening process.

54% of the employers chose not to hire candidates due to what they saw on their social media profiles. And even after landing that job, you are still not free from scrutiny.

The same study showed that 51% of employers monitor their employees' posts to make sure they aren't breaking the law, sharing confidential information, or harassing their fellow employees. There are many cases of people who've lost their jobs because of their social media posts or profiles.

Take, for instance, the popular case of Justine Sacco, who, in 2013, was traveling to South Africa. She posted, "Going to Africa. [I] hope I don't get AIDS. Just kidding. I'm white!" She only had 170 followers at that time, but she trended worldwide,[19] and by the time she was landing In South Africa, she had already gotten a note from her manager saying they'd fired her.

That shows you just how important a good online reputation is.

LinkedIn

LinkedIn is the most outstanding of all the professional platforms, and anybody that is somebody in the business world is on LinkedIn. Hence, having a LinkedIn profile makes you visible to top recruiters and decision-makers.

The Best Linkedin Practices And Top-Tier Profile Building Technics

Having a LinkedIn profile that stands out and that attracts your target audience can make all the difference. To do this, here're some ground rules you should adhere to and follow religiously:

#: Choose your best face

Your profile picture is the first thing people see when they click on your profile. For your profile picture, make sure it is professional, friendly, and approachable.

You might want to have your picture done by a professional photographer—it pays to go the extra mile. However, if you can't, go for a recent photo and ensure that your face is at the center of the frame—it should fill about 60% of the frame.

#: Describe yourself on your headline

Listing your job title on your headline is okay, but do you think this makes for a strong first impression? Let your headline sum up what you do in just a few catchy words. Make it memorable and unique.

An example of such a headline is:

FIG2: SAMPLE LINKEDIN HEADLINE FROM LINKEDIN BUSINESS [20]

#: Tell your story with the summary

Regular generalized summaries don't tell people who you are, what you have to offer, and your passion for your work. All these are essential to building trust with new clients or employers.

For the perfect summary:

- Don't be overly formal

- Write in the first person

- Make it about you, your goals, and your passions

- Just be yourself—it will sound more natural.

Also, avoid or limit commonly used words such as creative, motivated, passionate, successful, etc. They only harm your authenticity and don't add much value to your profile.

#: Have references to build your credibility

Everyone wants to work with someone they can trust. There is no better way to earn trust than showing people that you are good at what you do. Collect references from people that can describe your experience in the best way possible. Ask your referees to be as detailed as possible with their recommendations.

#: Showcase yourself

You should have at least five skills listed on your profile- people with such skills get 17 times more[21] profile clicks. The skills you list should be specific to your industry. Ensure you also keep your skillset updated—in case you change careers, acquire new competencies, take up new tasks, etc.

Profile Optimization

In addition to creating a profile that stands out, ensure that you make your profile work for you, not against you. Optimize your profile to ensure your target audience can easily find it.

The first thing you need to optimize is your profile by securing your vanity URL. To create this URL, you simply need to use both your first name and last. If your name is common and isn't available, you can include your middle name or the initial. Consistency in your brand name across platforms is essential for success.

It helps you build a reliable name and image for yourself. Before finalizing your URL, check if this name is available on other social media platforms. A tool such as Namechk [22] can help you with this.

You will also need to throw in industry keywords in your summary, job title, and headline. As LinkedIn is one of the largest databases of contacts, you will need to find a way to make yourself visible. The keywords you list will help you with this. The trick is to be as specific as you can and avoid generic titles.

Growing A Linkedin Community

With the perfect profile created, it is time to grow your LinkedIn community. You can do this by:

- **Joining groups:** There is something for everyone on LinkedIn. Search for groups you have an interest in and groups that relate to your specific industry. Don't just join groups; make sure you participate too! Share content, engage in discussions, view jobs, etc.

- **Invite your contacts:** I'm pretty sure most of your existing contacts are on LinkedIn already, so it's a matter of inviting them to connect with you digitally. You can either import your address book or manually search for your contact names on the platform.

- **Invite possible contacts:** As you frequently interact with people on LinkedIn (directly or indirectly), you will be able to make new connections every month. To check for potential contacts, you can click on the 'My Network' section, choose Connections, and they will appear there. You can also use the 'People You May Know' feature for the same.

Become An Authority

Nothing says, "I know what I'm doing," like creating something entirely original. Such creativity makes you stand out; it makes you unique, something you need to achieve career and professional growth.

For the sake of building your brand, you can create a blog or write a book, whichever sits right with you.

Create a blog

If you chose to create a blog, ensure that whatever you post somehow aligns with your career and what you love doing.

A blog should give you a sense of satisfaction. If you aren't excited to sit down and come up with a blog post, you need to change your content. A blog is great for your career growth because it:

#: Boosts your professional profile

Blogging will give potential employers something concrete about your expertise, which is why you should make sure your content is current and not random. The blog's whole point is to show recruiters how much you know, what you think, and how that value translates to them.

Even with limited experience, this is a great way to sell your brand because you can do ample research and offer solutions to show just how passionate and motivated you are about your chosen career path.

#: Can attract decision-makers

Imagine a situation where someone posts on their blog about an area of concern in their industry, and the blog post gets noticed and shared all over social media and other online articles. That's is the kind of exposure that can lead key decision makers to you.

#: Expands your network

There is only so much effort you can put into your networking efforts. Blogging helps you bring your target audience to you rather than having to go out of your way to look for them; it has the power to put you on the map. Just make sure to indicate your contact information and handles on your blog to make sure people can connect with you.

#: Boosts your resume

Employers are usually looking for reasons not to throw resumes in the "not sure" pile; they want to make final decisions as rapidly as possible. A blog compliments your resume and adds context to how well you apply your knowledge and skills.

#: Helps you build your skills

As you manage your blog, you will get the chance to learn new skills such as Search Engine Optimization (SEO), writing skills, use of analytical tools, social media navigating skills, and CMS, such as Word-

Press. Employers will undoubtedly consider these skills.

Blogging also authenticates you as a leader. When you are creating content that offers guidance, advice, and solutions, you are helping people. Besides showing you have good communication skills, it also shows that you love helping people.

In addition to these benefits, you can also monetize your blog by offering and selling coaching and consulting services, creating and selling online courses, earning affiliate income, etc.

Book publishing

Publishing a book is also a great way to boost your brand. Its benefits are similar to those you get from creating and sharing content on a blog.

When you decide to write and publish a book, opt for self-publishing on Amazon or use an online publishing agency; the latter is more convenient and gives you greater control over the creative process while the agency can manage your publishing, listings, and book marketing.

 You can also use your book to generate additional income if you decide to monetize it.

The Power of Twitter

With over 335 million users—at the time of writing this—Twitter is one of the most promising platforms for brands. This platform can help you reach a broad audience and connect with potential clients, employers, and your target audience in general.

Why is Twitter useful for your brand?

- It has over 335 million[23] active users.

- About 69 million of the users are US-based.

- At least 66% of organizations[24] in the US, with more than a hundred employees, use Twitter for marketing and interact with potential hires and clients.

More specifically, Twitter is essential for your brand because:

- ***You reach a wide audience hence are more visible:*** Twitter's large user base consists of different people with different needs for services, content, products, and so much more! All you need to do is put your content out there.

- ***You can showcase your work***: Twitter allows you to create threads and media attachments that you can use to showcase what you do best.

- ***You can create a brand identity***: When you are on Twitter, you can communicate your personality and ethos to make yourself appealing to your target audience.

- ***You get instant feedback***: Since you will be interacting with your target audience directly, they can communicate their thoughts about your brand, and from there, you can improve where necessary and do more of what is working.

Twitter Profile Optimization Tips

As a brand, you need to do everything you can to prove that you are human. That's because around 15%[25] of tweets are usually bots-posted. I don't think your target audience would prefer engaging with a bot.

Do everything in your power to make your profile more personal. Here are some ways you can do this:

- ***Using a clean profile picture:*** Your profile picture should be clear, and most of it should be your face—a headshot at that. You can also use a high-resolution brand logo if you have one.

- ***Location info, industry keywords, and relevant tags:*** In other words, your profile should have a complete description of what you do, your location, the company(s) you work with, and your title.

- ***A peek into your personality***: It is always a plus to give your followers a sense of who you are.

These tips can help you make a great first impression with your followers.

How To Grow A Twitter Community (And Best Practices)

A large following shows the influence you have in your industry of choice and that your target audience is interested in your content.

Without using spammy ploys and bots, here's how you can grow your Twitter following:

#: Tweet Often

Compared to its counterparts, Instagram and Facebook, Twitter requires you to be more aggressive with your content. Based on data by CoSchedule, the optimum number of tweets per day is between 3 and 7.[26] You don't have to just tweet about yourself. You can retweet tweets from followers, breaking news, articles relating to relevant industry, important stats, and so on. Just ensure to feed your followers with fresh content daily.

#: Check your timing

Blasting your timeline with tweets when your target audience is asleep won't help you grow your Twitter following. Sprout's research[27] shows that the best time to post on Twitter is usually during the weekdays in the early and late afternoons because this is when brands get the most engagement.

However, you should note that these numbers can vary depending on your audience and time zone.

If you aren't sure what time to tweet, you can use ViralPost,[28] which automatically schedules your tweets and posts them when your target audience is most likely to see and interact with them.

#: Get visual

Tweets featuring visual content—images, GIFs, or videos, infographics—are more appealing. They get more retweets, shares, and likes than tweets that lack the same.

As such, you should try to add a relevant, accompanying image for your tweets; there is nothing wrong with media-less tweets though, those with images are just more appealing.

#: Use those hashtags

Consider hashtags as a form of SEO for your Twitter account. Tweets with hashtags get 12.6% more engagement[29] than tweets without, so don't be afraid to get your hashtag on. Just make sure that the hashtags you use don't detract from the content.

To do this, you will need to find a way to include the hashtag in the tweet naturally. Here is an example of such hashtag use in a tweet:

"I create refreshing #Contentmarketing **blogposts for B2B Saas companies, and help individuals create their strategy on** @Wix, @CoSchedule, @JoinPF**"**

#: Link with followers on your network

Let me let you in on a simple trick to gaining more followers and increasing your visibility within seconds.

Most people usually hesitate to upload their contacts to any social media network. However, syncing your contacts with Twitter can help you gain some new followers from your existing network. If the contacts you've synced are on Twitter, your account has a greater chance of coming up as a suggestion on the 'Who to Follow' section.

#: Go beyond

The final strategy would be promoting your Twitter account beyond Twitter. You can casually place your handles on your blog, marketing emails, other socials, or other strategic places.

CHAPTER 6

BREAK FREE

No, this is not about quitting your job! However, statistics[30] show that most people are stressed and anxious about their jobs and afraid of losing them.

The whole purpose of this book is to make sure that you are living your passion fully and doing the job you love without worrying about losing it. As you live your dream job and do what you love, you don't have to be 100% financially dependent on salary. Having an extra income source eliminates most of the stress caused by the idea of losing your job.

Income Resources You Can Tap Into While Still Working

Some ways you can make some extra cash while still at work include:

Monetizing your blog

Remember those affiliate links I had mentioned earlier? Let's dive a bit deeper into how you can make money from them.

Affiliate marketing involves promoting products on your website in the articles you post. To do this, you need to find the right affiliate network to collaborate with based on the type of content you post.

However, you don't necessarily need to have a website. Affiliate marketing can be as easy as driving traffic to the said affiliate network.

How To Be An Affiliate Marketer

To launch your own affiliate marketing business, follow the following steps:

#: Choose a network

We have many affiliate networks, some of which relate to well-known companies such as Apple, Amazon, and Google. All these are great affiliates that pay reasonably well.

If you aren't new to the online world, you have probably heard of ClickBank,[31] one of the most popular and oldest affiliate networks. This billion-dollar company concentrates on digital products such as software, eBooks, and membership sites.

Consider selling such products as they offer higher commissions than physical products (about 10-75% plus). Digital informational products are also easier to sell because consumers get immediate gratification and access after purchase.

You can also work with individuals or companies directly. No matter who you chose as your affiliate network, make sure you two are a good fit for each other—in terms of the agreement and the products in question.

#: Research the affiliate products

As a new affiliate marketer, you need to have a sound understanding of the products you'll be dealing with and promoting to your audience.

The best thing you can do is choose a niche where you can easily make money online and that has a good number of vendors. Diving into such an industry gives you a wide selection of affiliate products to promote to your audience.

As you get started, limit yourself to 2-3 products to make sure you understand the products and work your way from there as you get comfortable. This way, you'll get an understanding of the products your audience responds to best and those they don't respond to at all.

#: Think about buying before promoting

Don't get me wrong; there's no obligation to buy all the products you are promoting. Nevertheless, owning and using the products is a great way to establish trust and credibility.

Buying a product and using it can help you write product reviews, which are also a great way of enhancing your credibility as a marketer. Be as detailed as possible if you use the product and get results from it.

#: Use social media to get more traffic

Finally, promote your products on all platforms; you can make videos to demonstrate usage of the products.

Create a YouTube channel

Creating a YouTube channel is also a great way to some extra income while you are still working. You can do it effortlessly after work, during weekends, or even during your lunch break! All you need to do is identify the kind of content you want to share—ideally, focus on sharing something you are passionate about (your expertise).

The obvious way to make money through YouTube is ad revenue. However, this isn't the only way. A YouTube channel can earn you money in the following ways:

#: You can become a YouTube partner

This program is how frequent YouTuber's access special features on YouTube. With this feature, you can access different income streams such as ads, premium subscription fees, Super Chat, merchandise shelf, and channel membership.

To join this program, you will need a minimum of 4,000 watch hours and 1,000 subscribers. That means you will first need to make your YouTube channel that successful. After you achieve these numbers, set up an AdSense_account and explore your new monetization features.

#: You can sell your products

Selling products you create is a viable way to earn

money on YouTube. Think about something unique you would want to sell. It could be clothing, a type of food, a book, organic products, or anything representing some connection between your audience and you.

When you settle on a product, you will need to create a separate website where your audience can get the product. Don't forget to promote your products in your videos.

#: You can create sponsored content

The good thing about sponsored content is that you don't have to give YouTube a cut. All you have to do is negotiate with the brand you are promoting, and from there, they pay you directly. All you need is to find a partner that you would want to work with and make a deal.

However, be sure to be transparent about your advertising. YouTube contains a visible disclosure section that will help you ensure that your viewers know you are advertising to them.

#: Direct pay

You can also get your fans to pay you directly by hosting live chats where they can use Super Chat[32], a feature where your fans make their comments more visible and pinned and highlighted for a certain amount of time depending on the amount they pay. You can also encourage your viewers to become premium subscribers or channel members.

Besides YouTube and affiliate marketing, you can also teach people what you know through online built training. All you need to do is think about what you have expertise in and comfortably teach it to other people. From here, create a suitable website for the same and provide content. You can also use YouTube to teach the same.

CHAPTER 7

ENJOY YOUR SUCCESS (CONCLUSION)

Congratulations on having made it to the end of this book. Thank you for going through this journey of career and self-development with me. I hope by now, you have a clear picture of what you need to do to achieve career growth and success and how to go about it.

Before I sign out, here is a quick word of advice on how to live a better, more fulfilling life:

Be mindful

Live a conscious life and live it at the moment; whatever you are doing, focus on that moment, now. If you are at work, be at work; if you are writing a blog post, focus on that only.

Being mindful makes us more productive and improves the quality of what we are doing. In other words, try to enjoy every moment of what you are doing.

Live healthily

Aim to live a healthy life, be it in your relationships, the food you eat, your activity level, and so on. Take care of yourself because you need to be in optimum health to achieve all your goals and aims.

Practice empathy

Finally, learn how to be empathetic. People go through battles that we have no way of seeing, so always be kind and try to put yourself in other people's shoes, no matter how they may make you feel. Doing this is especially important in the workplace if you want to forge good relationships with your coworkers.

That's it from me!

How'd You Enjoyed Reading What's Your Dream Job: A Complete Guide to Landing Your Dream Job, Building a World-Class Personal Brand, and Achieving Success in Business and Life?

I want to say thank you for purchasing and reading this book! I hope you enjoyed it and it's provided value to your life. If you enjoyed reading this book and found some benefit in it, I'd love your support and hope that you could take a moment to post a review on Amazon. I'd love to hear from you, even if you have feedback, as it'll help me ensure that I improve this book and others in the future.

[1] *https://so06.tci-thaijo.org/index.php/IJBS/article/view/521*

[2] *https://member.monster.com/*

[3] *https://linkfy.to/M5TzL*

[4] *https://www.linkedin.com/*

[5] *https://www.xing.com/en*

[6] *https://www.bark.com/en/us/*

[7] *https://www.opportunitynetwork.com/*

[8] *https://www.jobcase.com/*

[9] *https://www.goodreads.com/work/quotes/3155860-the-money-game*

[10] *https://testets.com/pages/Career-Test-FIRO-B-BRAND.php*

[11] *https://careertestswork.com/mycareer/index.php?main_page=take_free*

[12] *https://www.16personalities.com/free-personality-test*

[13] *https://www.mbtionline.com/en-US/Products/For-you*

[14] *https://www.surveymonkey.co.uk/r/stressedatwork*

[15] *http://www.totem-consulting.com/wp-content/uploads/2016/02/Drivers-Questionaire-1.pdf*

[16] *https://journals.sagepub.com/doi/abs/10.1177/1745691618804166*

[17] *https://www.open.edu/openlearn/ocw/mod/oucontent/view.php?id=28130§ion=2.1*

[18] *https://linkfy.to/AMkbI*

[19] *https://www.nytimes.com/2015/02/15/magazine/how-one-stupid-tweet-ruined-justine-saccos-life.html*

[20] *https://linkfy.to/VxakI*

[21] *https://www.inc.com/john-nemo/how-to-get-more-engagement-on-linkedin-according-to-linkedin.html*

[22] *http://namechk.com/*

[23] *https://blog.hootsuite.com/twitter-statistics/*

[24] *https://www.brandwatch.com/blog/44-twitter-stats/*

[25] *https://www.cnet.com/news/new-study-says-almost-15-*

percent-of-twitter-accounts-are-bots/

[26]   *https://coschedule.com/blog/how-often-to-post-on-social-media/*

[27]   *https://sproutsocial.com/insights/best-times-to-post-on-social-media/*

[28] *https://sproutsocial.com/features/viralpost/*

[29] *https://sproutsocial.com/insights/how-to-use-hashtags/*

[30]   *https://www.stress.org/42-worrying-workplace-stress-statistics*

[31] *https://www.clickbank.com/*

[32] *https://linkfy.to/bFORV*